PATTERSON PLACE PRESS

CONTENTS

Bonus pages for attaching photos, additional stories, etc.

Paternal Great-Great-Grandparents

Maternal Great-Great-Grandparents

Paternal Great-Grandparents

Maternal Great-Grandparents

Paternal Grandparents

Maternal Grandparents

Father

Mother

You live as long as you are remembered.
—RUSSIAN PROVERB

Paternal Great-Great-Grandparents

Maternal Great-Great-Grandparents

Paternal Great-Grandparents

Maternal Great-Grandparents

Paternal Grandparents

Maternal Grandparents

Father

Mother

Always remember your roots.
They are the foundation of your life
and the wings of your future.

FAMILY STORIES

SUGGESTIONS:
This is your chance to go beyond the name noted on the family tree. Tell stories that show the personality behind the name and bring that ancestor to life.

If there's a person that you never met or don't remember well yourself, do you remember any stories or tidbits that were told by other family members?

Don't worry so much as about keeping a person's story in chronological order. Bring the person to life by telling specific stories that show the character of the person. Were they a hard worker? Was there something they always said? Were they ornery as a child? Were they quick to laugh or love to tell funny stories? Do you know where or how they met their spouse? Include details of historical or national events to put the lives of your ancestors into context.

The story of

The story of

The story of

The story of

The story of

The story of

The story of

The story of

FAMILY TRADITIONS

SUGGESTIONS:
Note your family's holiday traditions,
birthday celebrations, names passed on through
generations, annual family vacation spots,
schools and colleges attended, churches,
groups, or clubs, occupations, etc.

FAMILY TRADITIONS

FAMILY TRADITIONS

_____

_____

_____

_____

_____

_____

_____

_____

_____

_____

_____

_____

_____

_____

_____

_____

_____

FAMILY TRADITIONS

FAMILY TRADITIONS

_____

_____

_____

_____

_____

_____

_____

_____

_____

_____

_____

_____

_____

_____

_____

_____

_____

FAMILY TRADITIONS

The Homes Where Our Ancestors Lived

Home is the heart of the family and future generations
may want to see where the stories of their ancestors
actually took place. Even if the home is no longer
standing, record as much detail as you can remember
as to the location of where a home once stood.

Use the notes section to record special memories you
may have. Did you ever visit the home? Are there any
special items in the house that you remember?

The Homes Where
Our Ancestors Lived

CITY/TOWN, STATE, ADDRESS IF KNOWN:

_____

WHO LIVED THERE:

_____

NOTES:

_____

_____

_____

_____

YEAR BUILT: IS IT STILL STANDING?

CITY/TOWN, STATE, ADDRESS IF KNOWN:

_____

WHO LIVED THERE:

_____

NOTES:

_____

_____

_____

YEAR BUILT: IS IT STILL STANDING?

The Homes Where
Our Ancestors Lived

CITY/TOWN, STATE, ADDRESS IF KNOWN:

_____

WHO LIVED THERE:

_____

NOTES:

_____

_____

_____

_____

YEAR BUILT: _____   IS IT STILL STANDING? _____

CITY/TOWN, STATE, ADDRESS IF KNOWN:

_____

WHO LIVED THERE:

_____

NOTES:

_____

_____

_____

_____

YEAR BUILT: _____   IS IT STILL STANDING? _____

THE HOMES WHERE
OUR ANCESTORS LIVED

CITY/TOWN, STATE, ADDRESS IF KNOWN:

_____

WHO LIVED THERE:

_____

NOTES:

_____

_____

_____

_____

YEAR BUILT: _____ IS IT STILL STANDING? _____

CITY/TOWN, STATE, ADDRESS IF KNOWN:

_____

WHO LIVED THERE:

_____

NOTES:

_____

_____

_____

_____

YEAR BUILT: _____ IS IT STILL STANDING? _____

The Homes Where
Our Ancestors Lived

CITY/TOWN, STATE, ADDRESS IF KNOWN:
_____

WHO LIVED THERE:
_____

NOTES:
_____
_____
_____
_____

YEAR BUILT: _____   IS IT STILL STANDING? _____

CITY/TOWN, STATE, ADDRESS IF KNOWN:
_____

WHO LIVED THERE:
_____

NOTES:
_____
_____
_____
_____

YEAR BUILT: _____   IS IT STILL STANDING? _____

The Homes Where
Our Ancestors Lived

CITY/TOWN, STATE, ADDRESS IF KNOWN:

_____

WHO LIVED THERE:

_____

NOTES:

_____

_____

_____

_____

YEAR BUILT: _____   IS IT STILL STANDING? _____

CITY/TOWN, STATE, ADDRESS IF KNOWN:

_____

WHO LIVED THERE:

_____

NOTES:

_____

_____

_____

_____

YEAR BUILT: _____   IS IT STILL STANDING? _____

The Homes Where
Our Ancestors Lived

CITY/TOWN, STATE, ADDRESS IF KNOWN:

WHO LIVED THERE:

NOTES:

YEAR BUILT: IS IT STILL STANDING?

CITY/TOWN, STATE, ADDRESS IF KNOWN:

WHO LIVED THERE:

NOTES:

YEAR BUILT: IS IT STILL STANDING?

The Homes Where
Our Ancestors Lived

CITY/TOWN, STATE, ADDRESS IF KNOWN:

_____

WHO LIVED THERE:

_____

NOTES:

_____

_____

_____

_____

YEAR BUILT: IS IT STILL STANDING?

CITY/TOWN, STATE, ADDRESS IF KNOWN:

_____

WHO LIVED THERE:

_____

NOTES:

_____

_____

_____

_____

YEAR BUILT: IS IT STILL STANDING?

Notes

Notes

CEMETERY RECORDS

SUGGESTIONS:
Make it easy for future generations to visit the
resting places of their ancestors. Include details
to make it easy to find family plots in larger cemeteries,
note any unique stones or inscriptions. If you need
help finding locations, search online databases.

Cemetery Records

NAME: BIRTH DATE: DEATH DATE:

CEMETERY NAME | LOCATION | PLOT #:

NAME: BIRTH DATE: DEATH DATE:

CEMETERY NAME | LOCATION | PLOT #:

NAME: BIRTH DATE: DEATH DATE:

CEMETERY NAME | LOCATION | PLOT #:

NAME: BIRTH DATE: DEATH DATE:

CEMETERY NAME | LOCATION | PLOT #:

NAME: BIRTH DATE: DEATH DATE:

CEMETERY NAME | LOCATION | PLOT #:

NAME: BIRTH DATE: DEATH DATE:

CEMETERY NAME | LOCATION | PLOT #:

Cemetery Records

NAME:

BIRTH DATE: DEATH DATE:

CEMETERY NAME | LOCATION | PLOT #:

NAME:

BIRTH DATE: DEATH DATE:

CEMETERY NAME | LOCATION | PLOT #:

NAME:

BIRTH DATE: DEATH DATE:

CEMETERY NAME | LOCATION | PLOT #:

NAME:

BIRTH DATE: DEATH DATE:

CEMETERY NAME | LOCATION | PLOT #:

NAME:

BIRTH DATE: DEATH DATE:

CEMETERY NAME | LOCATION | PLOT #:

NAME:

BIRTH DATE: DEATH DATE:

CEMETERY NAME | LOCATION | PLOT #:

Cemetery Records

NAME: BIRTH DATE: DEATH DATE:

CEMETERY NAME | LOCATION | PLOT #:

NAME: BIRTH DATE: DEATH DATE:

CEMETERY NAME | LOCATION | PLOT #:

NAME: BIRTH DATE: DEATH DATE:

CEMETERY NAME | LOCATION | PLOT #:

NAME: BIRTH DATE: DEATH DATE:

CEMETERY NAME | LOCATION | PLOT #:

NAME: BIRTH DATE: DEATH DATE:

CEMETERY NAME | LOCATION | PLOT #:

NAME: BIRTH DATE: DEATH DATE:

CEMETERY NAME | LOCATION | PLOT #:

Cemetery Records

NAME: BIRTH DATE: DEATH DATE:

CEMETERY NAME | LOCATION | PLOT #:

NAME: BIRTH DATE: DEATH DATE:

CEMETERY NAME | LOCATION | PLOT #:

NAME: BIRTH DATE: DEATH DATE:

CEMETERY NAME | LOCATION | PLOT #:

NAME: BIRTH DATE: DEATH DATE:

CEMETERY NAME | LOCATION | PLOT #:

NAME: BIRTH DATE: DEATH DATE:

CEMETERY NAME | LOCATION | PLOT #:

NAME: BIRTH DATE: DEATH DATE:

CEMETERY NAME | LOCATION | PLOT #:

Cemetery Records

NAME: _____ BIRTH DATE: _____ DEATH DATE: _____

CEMETERY NAME | LOCATION | PLOT #:

_____

NAME: _____ BIRTH DATE: _____ DEATH DATE: _____

CEMETERY NAME | LOCATION | PLOT #:

_____

NAME: _____ BIRTH DATE: _____ DEATH DATE: _____

CEMETERY NAME | LOCATION | PLOT #:

_____

NAME: _____ BIRTH DATE: _____ DEATH DATE: _____

CEMETERY NAME | LOCATION | PLOT #:

_____

NAME: _____ BIRTH DATE: _____ DEATH DATE: _____

CEMETERY NAME | LOCATION | PLOT #:

_____

NAME: _____ BIRTH DATE: _____ DEATH DATE: _____

CEMETERY NAME | LOCATION | PLOT #:

_____

Cemetery Records

NAME: BIRTH DATE: DEATH DATE:

CEMETERY NAME | LOCATION | PLOT #:

NAME: BIRTH DATE: DEATH DATE:

CEMETERY NAME | LOCATION | PLOT #:

NAME: BIRTH DATE: DEATH DATE:

CEMETERY NAME | LOCATION | PLOT #:

NAME: BIRTH DATE: DEATH DATE:

CEMETERY NAME | LOCATION | PLOT #:

NAME: BIRTH DATE: DEATH DATE:

CEMETERY NAME | LOCATION | PLOT #:

NAME: BIRTH DATE: DEATH DATE:

CEMETERY NAME | LOCATION | PLOT #:

CEMETERY RECORDS

NAME: BIRTH DATE: DEATH DATE:

CEMETERY NAME | LOCATION | PLOT #:

NAME: BIRTH DATE: DEATH DATE:

CEMETERY NAME | LOCATION | PLOT #:

NAME: BIRTH DATE: DEATH DATE:

CEMETERY NAME | LOCATION | PLOT #:

NAME: BIRTH DATE: DEATH DATE:

CEMETERY NAME | LOCATION | PLOT #:

NAME: BIRTH DATE: DEATH DATE:

CEMETERY NAME | LOCATION | PLOT #:

NAME: BIRTH DATE: DEATH DATE:

CEMETERY NAME | LOCATION | PLOT #:

Cemetery Records

NAME: BIRTH DATE: DEATH DATE:

_____   _____   _____

CEMETERY NAME | LOCATION | PLOT #:

_____

NAME: BIRTH DATE: DEATH DATE:

_____   _____   _____

CEMETERY NAME | LOCATION | PLOT #:

_____

NAME: BIRTH DATE: DEATH DATE:

_____   _____   _____

CEMETERY NAME | LOCATION | PLOT #:

_____

NAME: BIRTH DATE: DEATH DATE:

_____   _____   _____

CEMETERY NAME | LOCATION | PLOT #:

_____

NAME: BIRTH DATE: DEATH DATE:

_____   _____   _____

CEMETERY NAME | LOCATION | PLOT #:

_____

NAME: BIRTH DATE: DEATH DATE:

_____   _____   _____

CEMETERY NAME | LOCATION | PLOT #:

_____

Notes

Notes

Notes

FAMILY HEIRLOOMS

SUGGESTIONS:
Use the "notes" section to indicate your wishes for
the item in the future (passed on to a certain
family member, donated to a museum, etc.)

Note the value of the item if you've had it appraised
and where appraisal paperwork can be found.

Use the back pages to paste photos of the treasures in
the book to avoid confusion if you have similar items.

Just for fun, research the item and find the
original manufacturer or selling price.

Group smaller items such as letters or postcards in
photo boxes (which can found in most craft stores).
Label the boxes then use a page to describe what's in
each box and their significance.

Family Heirlooms

ITEM DESCRIPTION:

_____

_____

_____

LOCATION:

_____

ORIGINALLY BELONGED TO:

_____

_____

YEAR OR DECADE BOUGHT OR USED:

_____

INTERESTING OR FUN FACTS OR MEMORIES ABOUT THIS ITEM:

_____

_____

_____

_____

_____

_____

_____

Notes: _____

_____

_____

_____

Family Heirlooms

ITEM DESCRIPTION:

_____

_____

_____

LOCATION:

_____

ORIGINALLY BELONGED TO:

_____

_____

YEAR OR DECADE BOUGHT OR USED:

_____

INTERESTING OR FUN FACTS OR MEMORIES ABOUT THIS ITEM:

_____

_____

_____

_____

_____

_____

_____

Notes: _____

_____

_____

_____

Family Heirlooms

ITEM DESCRIPTION:

_____

_____

_____

LOCATION:

_____

ORIGINALLY BELONGED TO:

_____

_____

YEAR OR DECADE BOUGHT OR USED:

_____

INTERESTING OR FUN FACTS OR MEMORIES ABOUT THIS ITEM:

_____

_____

_____

_____

_____

_____

_____

Notes: _____

_____

_____

_____

Family Heirlooms

ITEM DESCRIPTION:

_____

_____

_____

LOCATION:

_____

ORIGINALLY BELONGED TO:

_____

_____

YEAR OR DECADE BOUGHT OR USED:

_____

INTERESTING OR FUN FACTS OR MEMORIES ABOUT THIS ITEM:

_____

_____

_____

_____

_____

_____

_____

Notes: _____

_____

_____

_____

Family Heirlooms

ITEM DESCRIPTION:

_____

_____

_____

LOCATION:

_____

ORIGINALLY BELONGED TO:

_____

_____

YEAR OR DECADE BOUGHT OR USED:

_____

INTERESTING OR FUN FACTS OR MEMORIES ABOUT THIS ITEM:

_____

_____

_____

_____

_____

_____

_____

_____

Notes: _____

_____

_____

_____

Family Heirlooms

ITEM DESCRIPTION:

_____

_____

_____

LOCATION:

_____

ORIGINALLY BELONGED TO:

_____

_____

YEAR OR DECADE BOUGHT OR USED:

_____

INTERESTING OR FUN FACTS OR MEMORIES ABOUT THIS ITEM:

_____

_____

_____

_____

_____

_____

_____

Notes: _____

_____

_____

_____

Family Heirlooms

ITEM DESCRIPTION:

_____

_____

_____

LOCATION:

_____

ORIGINALLY BELONGED TO:

_____

_____

YEAR OR DECADE BOUGHT OR USED:

_____

INTERESTING OR FUN FACTS OR MEMORIES ABOUT THIS ITEM:

_____

_____

_____

_____

_____

_____

_____

Notes: _____

_____

_____

_____

Family Heirlooms

ITEM DESCRIPTION:

_____

_____

_____

LOCATION:

_____

ORIGINALLY BELONGED TO:

_____

_____

YEAR OR DECADE BOUGHT OR USED:

_____

INTERESTING OR FUN FACTS OR MEMORIES ABOUT THIS ITEM:

_____

_____

_____

_____

_____

_____

_____

Notes: _____

_____

_____

_____

Family Heirlooms

ITEM DESCRIPTION:

_____

_____

_____

LOCATION:

_____

ORIGINALLY BELONGED TO:

_____

_____

YEAR OR DECADE BOUGHT OR USED:

_____

INTERESTING OR FUN FACTS OR MEMORIES ABOUT THIS ITEM:

_____

_____

_____

_____

_____

_____

_____

Notes: _____

_____

_____

_____

Family Heirlooms

ITEM DESCRIPTION:

_____

_____

_____

LOCATION:

_____

ORIGINALLY BELONGED TO:

_____

_____

YEAR OR DECADE BOUGHT OR USED:

_____

INTERESTING OR FUN FACTS OR MEMORIES ABOUT THIS ITEM:

_____

_____

_____

_____

_____

_____

_____

Notes: _____

_____

_____

_____

Family Heirlooms

ITEM DESCRIPTION:

_____

_____

LOCATION:

_____

ORIGINALLY BELONGED TO:

_____

_____

YEAR OR DECADE BOUGHT OR USED:

_____

INTERESTING OR FUN FACTS OR MEMORIES ABOUT THIS ITEM:

_____

_____

_____

_____

_____

_____

_____

Notes: _____

_____

_____

Family Heirlooms

Item Description:

_____

_____

Location:

_____

Originally belonged to:

_____

_____

Year or decade bought or used:

_____

Interesting or fun facts or memories about this item:

_____

_____

_____

_____

_____

_____

Notes: _____

_____

_____

_____

Family Heirlooms

ITEM DESCRIPTION:

_____

_____

_____

LOCATION:

_____

ORIGINALLY BELONGED TO:

_____

_____

YEAR OR DECADE BOUGHT OR USED:

_____

INTERESTING OR FUN FACTS OR MEMORIES ABOUT THIS ITEM:

_____

_____

_____

_____

_____

_____

_____

Notes: _____

_____

_____

_____

Family Heirlooms

ITEM DESCRIPTION:

_____

_____

_____

LOCATION:

_____

ORIGINALLY BELONGED TO:

_____

_____

YEAR OR DECADE BOUGHT OR USED:

_____

INTERESTING OR FUN FACTS OR MEMORIES ABOUT THIS ITEM:

_____

_____

_____

_____

_____

_____

_____

Notes: _____

_____

_____

_____

Family Heirlooms

ITEM DESCRIPTION:

_____

_____

_____

LOCATION:

_____

ORIGINALLY BELONGED TO:

_____

_____

YEAR OR DECADE BOUGHT OR USED:

_____

INTERESTING OR FUN FACTS OR MEMORIES ABOUT THIS ITEM:

_____

_____

_____

_____

_____

_____

_____

Notes: _____

_____

_____

_____

Family Heirlooms

ITEM DESCRIPTION:

_____

_____

_____

LOCATION:

_____

ORIGINALLY BELONGED TO:

_____

_____

YEAR OR DECADE BOUGHT OR USED:

_____

INTERESTING OR FUN FACTS OR MEMORIES ABOUT THIS ITEM:

_____

_____

_____

_____

_____

_____

_____

Notes: _____

_____

_____

_____

Family Recipes

Suggestions:
Use the "notes" pages for anecdotes about family
food traditions, the families' best and worst cooks,
or notes on where to find hard-to-find ingredients.

Title: _____

From the kitchen of: _____

INGREDIENTS:

DIRECTIONS:

Title: _____

From the kitchen of: _____

INGREDIENTS:

DIRECTIONS:

Title: _____

From the kitchen of: _____

INGREDIENTS:

DIRECTIONS:

Title: _____

From the kitchen of: _____

INGREDIENTS:

DIRECTIONS:

Title:

From the kitchen of:

INGREDIENTS: DIRECTIONS:

Title:

From the kitchen of:

INGREDIENTS: DIRECTIONS:

Title: _____

From the kitchen of: _____

INGREDIENTS:

DIRECTIONS:

Title: _____

From the kitchen of: _____

INGREDIENTS:

DIRECTIONS:

Title: _____

From the kitchen of: _____

INGREDIENTS:

_____
_____
_____
_____
_____
_____
_____
_____
_____
_____

DIRECTIONS:

_____
_____
_____
_____
_____
_____
_____
_____
_____
_____
_____

Title: _____

From the kitchen of: _____

INGREDIENTS:

_____
_____
_____
_____
_____
_____
_____
_____
_____
_____

DIRECTIONS:

_____
_____
_____
_____
_____
_____
_____
_____
_____
_____
_____

Title: _____

From the kitchen of: _____

INGREDIENTS:

DIRECTIONS:

Title: _____

From the kitchen of: _____

INGREDIENTS:

DIRECTIONS:

Title: _____

From the kitchen of: _____

INGREDIENTS:

DIRECTIONS:

Title: _____

From the kitchen of: _____

INGREDIENTS:

DIRECTIONS:

Title: _____

From the kitchen of: _____

INGREDIENTS:

_____
_____
_____
_____
_____
_____
_____
_____
_____
_____

DIRECTIONS:

_____
_____
_____
_____
_____
_____
_____
_____
_____
_____
_____
_____

Title: _____

From the kitchen of: _____

INGREDIENTS:

_____
_____
_____
_____
_____
_____
_____
_____
_____

DIRECTIONS:

_____
_____
_____
_____
_____
_____
_____
_____
_____

Title: _____

From the kitchen of: _____

INGREDIENTS:

DIRECTIONS:

Title: _____

From the kitchen of: _____

INGREDIENTS:

DIRECTIONS:

Notes

Notes

IMPORTANT DOCUMENTS

ITEM: LOCATION:

_____   _____

_____   _____

_____   _____

_____   _____

_____   _____

_____   _____

_____   _____

_____   _____

_____   _____

_____   _____

_____   _____

_____   _____

_____   _____

_____   _____

_____   _____

_____   _____

_____   _____

_____   _____

ITEM:

LOCATION:

Remember
THOSE WHO CAME BEFORE YOU

Treasure
THE KEEPSAKES LEFT BEHIND

I LOVE THE THINGS THAT HAVE HISTORY...
things well loved and well cared for

Made in United States
Troutdale, OR
11/19/2024

25046525R00058